# STEM IN CURRENT EVENTS

▸ Agriculture ▸ Energy ▸ Entertainment Industry ▸ Environment & Sustainability
▸ Forensics ▸ Information Technology ▸ Medicine and Health Care
▾ **Space Science** ▸ Transportation ▸ War and the Military

# SPACE SCIENCE

▶ Floating in the Space Station

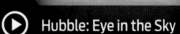

▶ Hubble: Eye in the Sky

▶ Private Spacecraft: Wave of the Future?

## STEM IN CURRENT EVENTS

Agriculture

Energy

Entertainment Industry

Environment & Sustainability

Forensics

Information Technology

Medicine and Health Care

Space Science

Transportation

War and the Military

# SPACE SCIENCE

By John Perritano

WITHDRAWN

**Mason Crest**
450 Parkway Drive, Suite D
Broomall, PA 19008
www.masoncrest.com

© 2017 by Mason Crest, an imprint of National Highlights, Inc.

Printed and bound in the United States of America.

First printing
9 8 7 6 5 4 3 2 1

Series ISBN: 978-1-4222-3587-4
Hardback ISBN: 978-1-4222-3595-9
ebook ISBN: 978-1-4222-8296-0

Produced by Shoreline Publishing Group
*Designer:* Tom Carling, Carling Design Inc.
*Production:* Sandy Gordon
www.shorelinepublishing.com

Front cover: NASA (3)

Library of Congress Cataloging-in-Publication Data

Names: Perritano, John.
Title: Space science / by John Perritano.
Description: Broomall, PA : Mason Crest, [2017] |
Series: STEM in current    events | Includes index.
Identifiers: LCCN 2016004810| ISBN 9781422235959 (hardback) | ISBN    9781422235874 (series) | ISBN
    9781422282960 (ebook)
Subjects:  LCSH: Space sciences--Juvenile literature.
Classification: LCC QB500.22 .P47 2017 | DDC 500.5--dc23
LC record available at http://lccn.loc.gov/2016004810

# Contents

Introduction: Life on Mars? ....................................................................6

**1** Science and Space .....................................................................14

**2** Technology and Space ...........................................................30

**3** Engineering and Space ..........................................................42

**4** Math and Space ......................................................................54

Find Out More.................................................................................62

Series Glossary of Key Terms.......................................................63

Index/Author ................................................................................ 64

## Key Icons to Look For

 **Words to Understand:** These words with their easy-to-understand definitions will increase the reader's understanding of the text, while building vocabulary skills.

 **Sidebars:** This boxed material within the main text allows readers to build knowledge, gain insights, explore possibilities, and broaden their perspectives by weaving together additional information to provide realistic and holistic perspectives.

 **Educational Videos:** Readers can view videos by scanning our QR codes, providing them with additional educational content to supplement the text. Examples include news coverage, moments in history, speeches, iconic sports moments, and much more!

 **Text-Dependent Questions:** These questions send the reader back to the text for more careful attention to the evidence presented here.

 **Research Projects:** Readers are pointed toward areas of further inquiry connected to each chapter. Suggestions are provided for projects that encourage deeper research and analysis.

 **Series Glossary of Key Terms:** This back-of-the-book glossary contains terminology used throughout this series. Words found here increase the reader's ability to read and comprehend higher-level books and articles in this field.

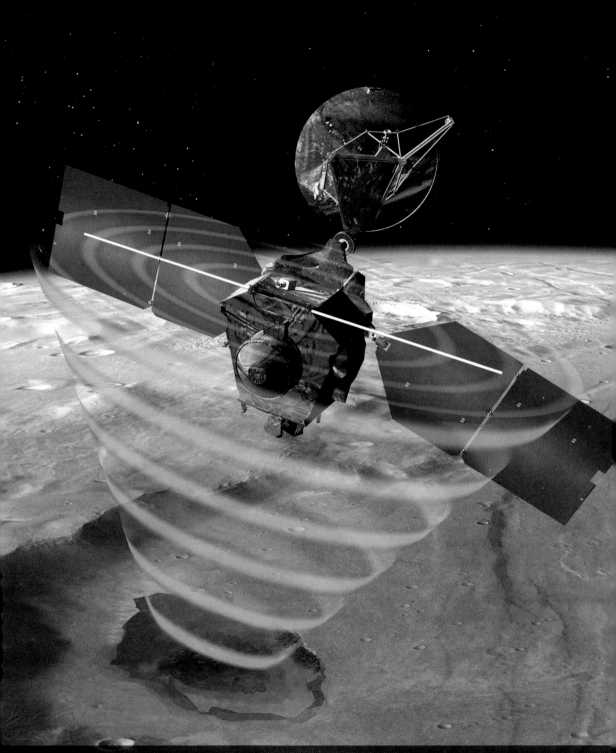

This artist's conception shows how the Mars Reconnaissance Orbiter used ground-penetrating radar to discover evidence of water beneath the surface of the planet.

# INTRODUCTION
# Life on Mars?

## Words to Understand

**acronym**   a word formed from the initials or other parts of several words

**hydrated**   combined with water

**radiation**   energy emitted in the form of tiny particles whose atoms are not stable and are decaying

**striations**   striped patterns; banding with grooves that are narrow and parallel

In September 2015, scientists at NASA, the space agency of the United States, made a startling announcement. One of their spaceships, the Mars Reconnaissance Orbiter (MRO), found evidence of water flowing on the surface of the Red Planet. The orbiter didn't find a river or an ocean, but **striations** in rock created by **hydrated** salt that only rushing water could have created.

The news rocked the world, because where there is water, scientists said, there might be life. "Our quest on Mars has been to 'follow the water' in our search for life in the universe, and now

Computers combined several images from MRO to illustrate what this slope on the inside of a crater would look like over time, showing flows of material down its sides.

we have convincing science that validates what we've long suspected," said John Grunsfeld, a U.S. astronaut and NASA official.

Earthlings have studied Mars since ancient times, and for nearly half a century our machines have traveled to the planet to learn as much as they can. Some, like the Mars Reconnaissance Orbiter, circled Mars from above. Others were robotic rovers that crisscrossed the planet's surface.

Ten years of Mars Reconnaissance Orbiter

Although Mars is the most studied planet in our solar system (with the exception of Earth, of course), humans have yet to set foot there. The discovery of water, however, amped up calls for us to visit and perhaps colonize the world that the ancient Egyptians called "Har Decher"—the "Red One." And if we did, where would we live?

NASA scientists have asked that question many times, which is why they encouraged engineers to come up with a plan for a human habitat that uses the planet's natural resources and 3D printing technology.

Why such a combination? As the movie *The Martian* underscored, living and working on Mars would be a challenging and dangerous experience. Once on the surface, humans would need to be there for an extended period. They would have to find ways to use what they found on the planet to survive, including raw materials to build their own shelters.

# Bubble-Shaped Igloo

That's where 3D printing comes into play. Also known as additive manufacturing, 3D printing allows people to use different materials to create, or "print" objects, including toys, cell phone cases, spare parts for a car, or a house. The printers can build such items out of plastic, metal, or, in the case of a Martian apartment building, iron dust and ice.

With that in mind, French engineers designed a 3D habitat made out of iron oxide, the most abundant mineral on Mars, and the one responsible for giving the planet its reddish tint. The French call their bubble-shaped home Sfero, an **acronym** for the French words sphere, iron, and water. Engineers designed the abode to house four people in 861 square feet (80 sq m) of space.

The habitat has three floors—two below ground, one above—connected by a spiral staircase. An airlock connects the above ground level to the outside. In addition to sleeping and living quarters, the engineers designed Sfero with storage, recreation, and indoor garden areas.

**Carbon Copies**

Here on Earth, people are building 3D structures all the time. A Chinese company used its 3D printer to build 10 single-story houses in one day. The houses were printed from a cement-based mixture that contained construction waste and glass fibers. Each house cost about $5,000 to build.

At the heart of Sfero is a robotic mast that can drill into the planet's frozen soil. Once anchored, the mast deploys two arms, allowing it to mine for iron oxide. The 3D printer will then use the mineral to manufacture each section of the habitat one piece at a time. As each part is "printed," astronauts would put the structure together like a big jigsaw puzzle.

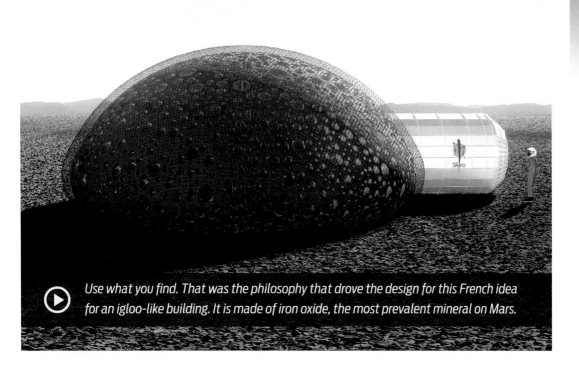

Use what you find. That was the philosophy that drove the design for this French idea for an igloo-like building. It is made of iron oxide, the most prevalent mineral on Mars.

"We can build everything with 3D printing, right down to the closet hinges," said Arnault Coulet, whose 3D printing company imagined the idea.

## Mars Ice House

Using iron oxide is one way to build a Martian house. Using water is another way. Engineers from the United States and Japan envision constructing a 3D Ice House on Mars. The sloping pyramid-shaped building would not be your average igloo, but one that acts as a shield to protect astronauts and their gardens from space **radiation**.

Is this the future? The astronaut drawn toward the bottom right shows the scale of one design for a future moon or extraterrestrial habitat for humans.

"The advantage of 3D printing is that we can do everything on site and take advantage of the resources on hand, namely iron and water in the form of ice," said Pierre Brisson, a member of the Mars Society, a group that wants humans to one day colonize the planet.

## Science Fiction, No More

When it comes to outer space, 3D printing technology is just one of the latest tools scientists hope to one day use to turn science fiction into science reality. Some scientists and engineers are working every day to find new ways to travel to distant planets and stars, while other use super-powerful telescopes to look back in time to understand how the universe was created. Still others design space probes that can catch up to a streaking comet or asteroid in the hopes of finding the molecules of life.

With all this knowledge, colonizing Mars may one day be in our grasp, and then, perhaps, traveling to a distant galaxy light years away.

"We see the stars, and we want them," science fiction author Ray Bradbury once said. "…If we make landfall on another star system, we become immortal."

# Text-Dependent Questions

1. What did the Mars Reconnaissance Orbiter find on Mars that led scientists to believe water is rushing on the Red Planet?

2. How do 3D printers work?

3. Which mineral would the Sfero robot use on Mars to build a habitat for humans?

# Research Project

Work in groups of three or four and design a habitat that humans can use on Mars. You can use a computer or draw the habitat freehand. Your design should include living quarters, a work area, a recreation area, and indoor gardens.

The Hubble Space Telescope created this image of the Butterfly Nebula. By giving scientists from many fields a closer look at deep space, Hubble has literally opened new horizons in space science.

# SCIENCE AND
# Space

## 1

## Words to Understand

**cyanobacteria**   oxygen-producing bacteria that can make their own food

**genomes**   a full set of genetic information that an organism inherits from its ancestors

**interstellar**   moving between stars

**synthesize**   produce new substances by a chemical or biological process

Space is a place of mystery and wonder. It tells us where we've been and where we hope to go. Science has allowed us to peer back nearly 13.7 billion years to when the universe was born. It has also allowed our telescopes to see distant galaxies that are no more than tiny smudges in the night sky. We have seen evidence of distant planets orbiting their suns, and found traces of dense black holes in galaxies far away.

Yet, the moon is the farthest place humans have traveled. While some of our probes and robots have rocketed to the edge of our solar system, we humans have been stuck in our own backyard. It's not because we don't want to leave. It's just that the laws of physics make it hard to go anywhere. Even if we can muster enough rocket power to shake off our earthly shackles, the universe is so vast that any trip from here to there would take a long time.

## Transforming Planets

That is why scientists are diligently trying to find ways to make **interstellar** travel a reality. Many believe the best way to travel through the vastness of space is to create ports of call linking one location to another just as seafaring explorers did centuries

*This series of images shows how a Mars-like planet might be terraformed over time to become one with water and an atmosphere like Earth's.*

Exoplanets have been found throughout the Milky Way galaxy. Astronomers are searching for planets that might have conditions to support life as we know it.

ago. It's a process called terraforming. That means tinkering with an alien world's environment to make it habitable for human travelers. The goal is to engineer an environment that contains oxygen, water, and plant life, all of which are necessary for human survival.

Chris McKay is a scientist trying to find the best way to create an Earth-like environment on a distant world. McKay wants to terraform Mars, a barren rock that as far as we know is devoid of plant life, but encompasses many of the ingredients that could make life thrive on its surface.

"You don't build on Mars," McKay, a scientist at NASA's Ames Research Center told National Geographic. "You just warm it up and throw some seeds."

Sounds easy, but it's not. The best evidence suggests that Mars is a planet with all the necessary building blocks of life, includ-

 *Big ideas: What if all the water that is currently frozen at Mars' poles was to melt and spread around the planet? Would it be capable of supporting humans?*

ing carbon, oxygen, and water. The way to terraform Mars, McKay says, is to **synthesize** these materials to create a greenhouse effect that will warm the planet to the point where it can sustain life.

Warming Mars will allow carbon dioxide to escape from the planet's polar ice caps. As the gas evaporates, it will linger in the atmosphere, creating a thermal blanket that will trap the sun's heat close to the surface, just like a farmer's greenhouse. As the planet warms and its atmospheric pressure increases, liquid water will begin to flow as trapped ice melts.

One way to jump-start the process is to pump human-made perfluorocarbons (PFCs) into the Martian atmosphere. PFCs are a group of chemicals composed of carbon and fluorine. PFCs are supercharged greenhouse gases—it only takes a little to heat a planet. PFCs last for a long time, and unlike their distant cousins, chlorofluorocarbons, PFCs don't chew up an atmosphere's protective ozone layer. Ozone shields a planet from the sun's dangerous ultraviolet rays.

## Terraforming Venus

Some scientists believe that Venus, not Mars, would be the best candidate for terraforming. The atmosphere on Venus is made up mostly of carbon dioxide, which traps the sun's intense heat close to the surface. The gas makes Venus so hot that life as we know it cannot exist. Some propose shrouding Venus with giant sails to block the sun, cool its atmosphere, and cause carbon dioxide to fall to the surface. That, they say, would help life blossom.

But there is no water on Venus to sustain life. That's because all the hydrogen that was once on the planet drifted off into space when Venus formed. Water is made up in part of two hydrogen molecules. Scientists say it might be possible to divert comets toward the planet. Ice chunks from these dirty snowballs would break off and fall to the surface, seeding Venus with water molecules that could spur the creation of life.

Scientists are also studying ways to use **cyanobacteria** in terraforming. These oxygen-producing critters live in extreme environments on Earth, and were partly responsible for making Earth an oxygen-rich environment some 3.5 billion years ago. The bacteria make their own food, which means they don't have to rely on an alien world for lunch and dinner.

Once Mars begins to warm and the water begins to flow, humans will be able to seed the surface with plants and trees.

One of the major problems with terraforming is that it would take hundreds, if not thousands of years, to create ecosystems that can sustain human life. In fact, if humans were able to build 100 greenhouse-gas spewing factories on Mars, we would be able to warm the planet only six to eight degrees in 100 years. Mars is an extremely chilly planet, with an average temperature of minus-80°F (-60°C). At that rate, it would take 800 years or so to melt whatever ice there is on Mars.

"Devising more efficient artificial super-greenhouse gases will make it faster," said Margarita Marinova, who works with McKay.

## Genes and Space

Whether traveling to Mars, Pluto, or to some distant star system, humans will need to spend long stretches of time in outer space. Such a journey might have a negative impact on their bodies. As a result, astronauts will need to be able to sequence DNA to evaluate their own health and discover the makeup of new substances.

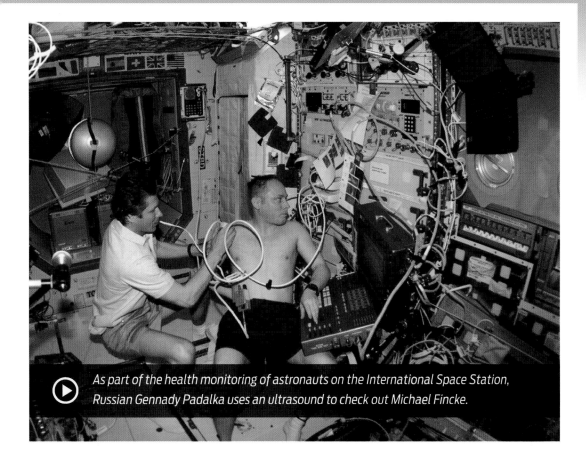

As part of the health monitoring of astronauts on the International Space Station, Russian Gennady Padalka uses an ultrasound to check out Michael Fincke.

DNA is short for deoxyribonucleic acid, a spiral-shaped molecule of chemicals containing a person's genes, the material that determines inherited characteristics such as eye and hair color. DNA is found in the body's cells.

Here on Earth, doctors use DNA technology to develop drugs and vaccines, and to reproduce human hormones and proteins, all of which could be important on long space voyages. Extracting DNA and using it to form other compounds is easy in normal Earth gravity, but no one has ever tried it in the weightlessness of space.

For three days in September 2015, Andrew Feinberg and Lindsay Rizzardi went on a weightless roller coaster of ride to see whether they could sequence DNA in zero gravity. Feinberg and Rizzardi, both geneticists at Johns Hopkins University in Baltimore, Maryland, climbed aboard a special NASA plane that creates artificial space. The plane flew high above the ground in a series of dips

Yes, that is famous physicist Stephen Hawking floating in zero gravity aboard the "Vomit Comet." The British scientist is confined to a wheelchair here on Earth.

and climbs that created brief periods of weightlessness. (The plane's nickname, the "Vomit Comet," comes from the nauseous effect such a flight can have on people.)

During the ride, Feinberg and Rizzardi tested two important tools they suspected would work differently in zero gravity than they do on Earth. Both are essential in extracting and sequencing DNA. During the first part of the experiment, the scientists tested several pipettes, thin tools that researchers use in the DNA extraction process. A pipette acts like a straw, allowing scientists to suck up a layer of body fluid and place it in another container.

The researchers knew it would be hard to move liquids in a weightless environment, which is why they tested three different liquid transfer methods. The first pipette they used had a long needle connected by plastic tubing. It didn't work very well. It was hard for Feinberg and Rizzardi to control the liquid's movement.

On their second try, Feinberg and Rizzardi used a standard pipette found in most DNA laboratories. However, that pipette created air bubbles, causing the liquid to climb up the sides of a container.

The third method worked perfectly. This time the researchers used a pipette that works like a syringe, similar to one used in vaccinations. That pipette did not create an air pocket between the plunger and the liquid, making it easier to transfer the solution.

The second experiment involved a pint-sized genetic sequencer called MinION. Most sequencers are big and bulky, but MinION is so small that it can fit into a suitcase. Scientists used the tiny

## Record-Setting Flight

On March 22, 1995, Russian cosmonaut Valeri Polyakov returned to Earth having spent 437 days in space. When he returned from the International Space Station, U.S. astronaut Norman Thagard said Polyakov looked "like he could wrestle a bear." Polyakov volunteered for the record-setting mission so scientists could study the impact of microgravity on humans during long space flights.

sequencer in 2014 to read the **genomes** of Ebola victims 48 hours after samples were collected.

Feinberg and Rizzardi tested the device as the Vomit Comet made its stomach-churning trip. They found it worked just as well in zero gravity as it did on the ground.

## Twin Study

Figuring out the best way to sequence DNA in the weightlessness of space is one of many problems geneticists are tackling. They also hope to learn how long spaceflights affect human DNA.

To that end, NASA astronaut Scott Kelly and his twin brother, former astronaut Mark Kelly, agreed to work with researchers hoping to shed light on the problem. On October 13, 2015, Scott Kelly set a new American record for spending the most time in space. At the time, Kelly was serving as the commander of the 45th crew to work aboard the International Space Station (ISS). As October 13 dawned aboard the ISS, Kelly had spent 381 days, 15 hours, and 11 minutes in Earth's orbit, including 180 days he had already spent in orbit on three previous missions.

Once Kelly returned to Earth, scientists planned to extract his DNA and compare it to his brother, who did not make the trip.

Among other things, researchers want to know whether cosmic rays—radiation from deep space—will shorten a person's life by damaging sections of DNA found at the end of every chromosome, the rod-shaped structure that carries genetic material, in a person's body.

Those DNA sections are like the plastic tips at the end of a shoelace that keep the fabric from splitting. Without the protective coverings, the ends of DNA strands can become damaged,

*Two for space: Twin NASA astronauts Scott (left) and Mark Kelly have devoted themselves to the study of life in space. Scott spent a year on the ISS.*

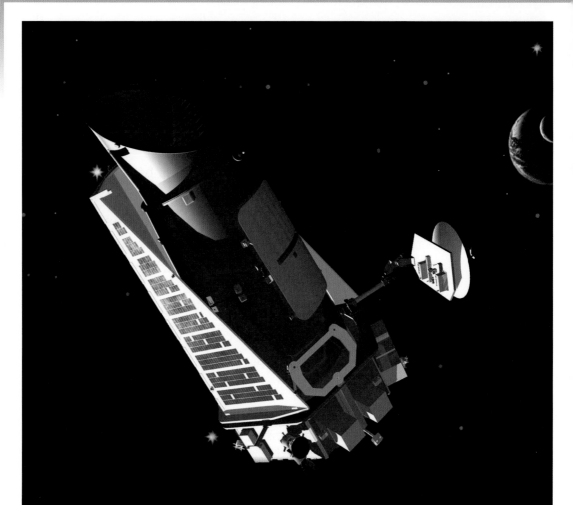

*This is an illustration of the Kepler Space Telescope that spins around Earth, beaming back amazing images and data about exoplanets.*

affecting the way a person ages. Scientists believe long space voyages amplify the effects of radiation and weightlessness and will cause Scott Kelly's "tips" to become shorter than those of his brother.

# "Bizarre Signals"

While some scientists try to figure the ins and outs of human space travel, others are content studying distant worlds. Many look for exoplanets that orbit stars thousands of light years away.

In 2009, NASA sent out the Kepler Space Telescope, hoping to find small, rocky worlds orbiting stars thousands of light years away. Kepler worked as planned. When the telescope detects an exoplanet, it sees the wobble of the planet as it orbits in front of a star. The telescope spots a slight dimming of starlight over time.

Planets are round, no matter where they are located, and each has a distinctive and predictable wobble. So when Kepler found something out of the ordinary a few years ago, scientists were forced to look deeper.

In the fall of 2015, researchers announced that Kepler found an unusual wobble as it peered at a star named KIC 8462852, located 1,500 light years from Earth. Kepler found that the dimming of the star was far too great to be caused by a planet crossing its path.

Researchers scratched their heads trying to figure out what was going on. They hypothesized, or made an educated guess, that a shattered comet veered off course toward KIC 8462852, jolted by a passing star. Others speculated that a gigantic dust cloud formed by the collision of two planets caused the weird wobble. Scientists dismissed both theories.

Their third theory, however, caused heads to turn. Scientists say the strange wobble could be caused by some "alien megastructure" orbiting the star. The anomaly was enough for astronomers at the SETI (Search for Extraterrestrial Intelligence) Institute to point the Allen Telescope Array, a system of radio telescopes northeast of San Francisco, toward the star in the hunt for intelligent radio signals.

Radio telescope dishes are always pointed to the sky, seeking signals, messages, or other communications that might be coming from worlds beyond ours.

Seth Shostak, a senior astronomer at SETI, told Space.com that people who want to support the alien structure theory should moderate their enthusiasm. "History suggests we're going to find an explanation for this that doesn't involve Klingons," he said.

# Text-Dependent Questions

1. Why do some scientists want to use cyanobacteria to terraform a planet?

2. What are genes, and why do scientists want to sequence them in outer space?

3. How does the Kepler Space Telescope detect planets orbiting distant stars?

# Research Project

Break off into groups and research more about terraforming. Next hold a debate to answer these questions: Should humans create Earth-like environments on other planets? What are the positive aspects of terraforming? What are the negative aspects?

*Three . . . two . . . one . . . blastoff! This Saturn V rocket was a key part of the 1960s Apollo missions that took men to the moon. Today's rockets are even more powerful, but also more efficient.*

# TECHNOLOGY AND
# Space

## 2

## Words to Understand

**carbonaceous** containing, or resembling, carbon

**cryogenic** at very low temperatures

**ions** electrically charged atoms

**isotopes** two or more forms of a chemical element, each having different numbers of neutrons

**neutron** an atomic particle with no electrical charge

**Z**ipping between worlds light years apart has always been a staple of good science fiction. In reality, or at least the reality in which we live today, journeying such vast distances is impracticable at best. Critics say the universe is too immense for interstellar space travel. Our spaceships just can't go fast enough to cover such distances in a reasonable amount of time.

What's a space traveler to do?

Researchers at NASA's Marshall Space Flight Center in Huntsville, Alabama, believe they have the answer: a propulsion system based on a nuclear reaction.

Most rocket systems use liquid fuel (generally hydrogen) and an oxidizer (oxygen) to create the energy needed to move through space. Each is stored at low temperatures in separate tanks of a rocket engine. When the two combine, they create a high-pressure, high-velocity stream of hot gases.

The result is an explosive effect that creates a tremendous amount of backward thrust that propels a rocket forward. The space shuttle's external liquid-fuel engine, for example, allowed the orbiter to speed along at 17,000 miles (27,358 km) per hour. At sea level, the main engine produced 375,000 pounds (179,097 kg) of thrust.

While those numbers might seem immense, they are not. Liquid-fuel chemical rockets have limited range. If we were to use the best rocket engines available today, it would take more than 50,000 years for humans to travel 4.3 light years to Alpha Centauri, the closest star to our sun. Light travels at 186,000 miles (299,337 km) per second. Moreover, there's just not enough fuel on Earth to propel a ship that far for that long.

A nuclear-powered rocket engine might not get us moving at the speed of light, but it would be more efficient than conventional engines. To that end, NASA's Huntsville Nuclear **Cryogenic** Propulsion Stage Team is using the latest in nuclear technology to heat hydrogen to extremely high temperatures. Scientists say the first nuclear cryogenic propulsion systems would be able to send a crew to Mars in less time than a conventional spacecraft. That would reduce human exposure to harmful space radiation.

The technology is simple. The upper stage of a nuclear cryogenic engine contains super-cold liquid hydrogen. Once outside Earth's atmosphere, a nuclear reactor super-heats the hydrogen. Then it forces it through a nozzle creating a massive amount of forward thrust. Nuclear engines would use less fuel and move the ship through space much faster than conventional rocket engines.

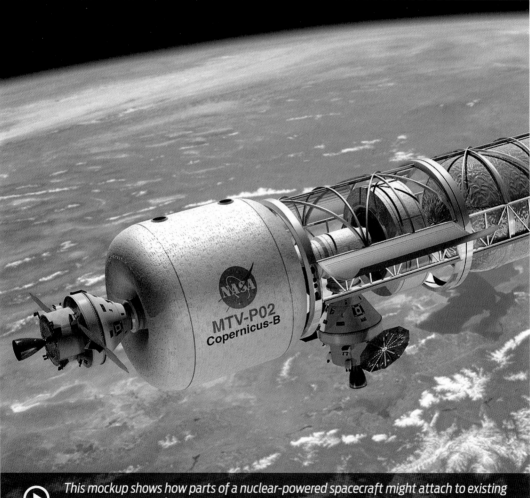

*This mockup shows how parts of a nuclear-powered spacecraft might attach to existing orbiting parts to help create space travel to new and more-distant worlds.*

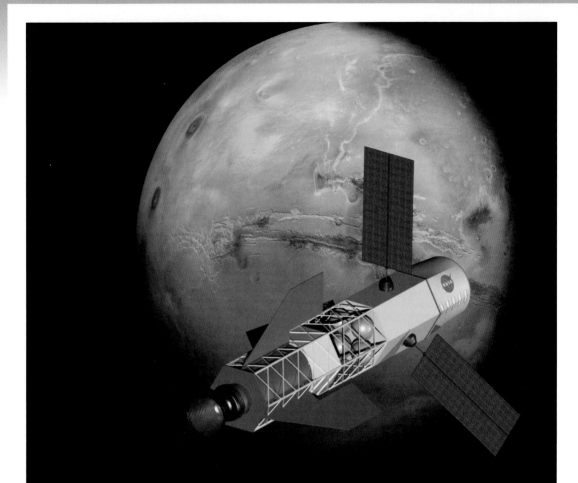

*The University of Washington's concept for a nuclear fusion-powered rocket is only on the drawing board, but it looks promising. Crew quarters are forward in this design.*

"The information we gain using this test facility will permit engineers to design rugged, efficient fuel elements and nuclear propulsion systems," said NASA researcher Bill Emrich, who manages the program at Marshall. "It's our hope that it will enable us to develop a reliable, cost-effective nuclear rocket engine in the not-too-distant future."

# Fusion Rockets

A Nuclear Cryogenic Propulsion Stage engine would obtain its power through a nuclear reaction called fission—the splitting of atoms. Fission occurs when a **neutron** from one atom hits the nucleus of another atom. As that happens, atoms release more neutrons that strike other atoms. As the atoms split, they spit out a huge amount of energy.

Yet, there is another type of nuclear reaction that could dwarf the power of a cryogenic engine: fusion. Instead of splitting atoms to create energy, fusion joins, or fuses, the nuclei of elements, creating massive amounts of energy.

Scientists are currently designing fusion-driven engines that use hydrogen as a propellant. By fusing heavy **isotopes** of hydrogen, just as the sun does to generate energy, a fusion-driven rocket can create an enormous amount of thrust and a vast amount of speed.

Scientists at the University of Washington are currently working on such an engine that they hope will cut travel time between Earth and Mars substantially.

## Project Orion

Using nuclear reactions as a means of propelling a rocket through space is not a new concept. In the 1950s, a group of scientists came up with an unusual scheme to use thousands of nuclear bombs to propel a spaceship the size of the Empire State Building to Mars, Saturn, and beyond. The idea was called Project Orion. Instead of using chemical liquid rocket fuel, the largest version of the Orion spaceship would have used thousands of exploding nuclear bombs to push the ship along.

The plan was far-fetched and downright scary. Still, it attracted some of the best minds in science, including Freeman Dyson, a theoretical physicist at the Institute for Advanced Study in Princeton, N.J., and Werner von Braun, who helped the United States put humans on the moon. Although scientists worked on the project for seven years, Orion never got off the ground.

## Solar Sails

Solar sails might provide the best way to propel a spaceship. Solar sails harness electrically charged particles emitted by the sun to move a spacecraft forward. Japan's *IKAROS* spacecraft was the first to use the technology in 2010. The spacecraft, which scientists sent on its way to Venus, is powered by individual light photons (packets of solar energy). As they hit the kite-shaped sail, the photons create enough energy to move the craft along. The sail is also stitched together with solar cells to generate electricity.

New fusion rocket: Mars in 30 days?

It currently takes about 500 days for a traditional chemical propulsion system rocket to make it to the Red Planet. The amount of time could be cut to 83 days if astronauts travel aboard a fusion-propelled ship.

The engine would rely on hydrogen plasma, a hot ionized gas made up of **ions** and electrons. The engine would inject bubbles of plasma into a chamber, where a magnetic field collapses the bubbles into a state in which they can be fused. The energy released by the nuclear reaction would be ejected out the back of the engine, pushing the spaceship on its way. Solar panels mounted on the outside of the ship would use the sun's rays to generate the electricity to keep the engine running.

"This is probably the most simple and straightforward, lowest-cost fusion propulsion system you can think of," John Slough, the project's lead, told Space.com. "The fundamental physics have been proven in the laboratory... so what I'm talking about is building a device with known physics and with a proven method."

# Chasing an Asteroid

Most of what we know about our solar system and the universe comes from robotic ships, rovers, satellites, telescopes, and other space machines. These unmanned probes have proved invalu-

*Have you ever seen a closeup image of a comet? Now you have. This is a composite image of 67P/Churyumov-Gerasimenko taken by the Rosetta spacecraft.*

able to scientific research. They can go where humans cannot. Some have driven across Mars or plumbed the deepest regions of our solar system. One probe even made an historic landing on a comet in 2014.

## Kepler Technology

Technology has allowed us to see things that we never guessed were there. When the Kepler Telescope was launched in 2009, scientists could only envision what galactic treasures it would find. One of its jobs was to see how many Earth-like planets might be out there. A few years later, we had an answer. To figure out this complicated bit of science, Kepler looked at a small slice of our home galaxy, the Milky Way. After carefully analyzing the data Kepler gleaned, then taking that information to include the entire galaxy, researchers say there are at least 8.8 billion stars with Earth-like size planets revolving around them.

Those planets, the researchers said, revolve around their suns in a so-called Goldilocks Zone, where life as we know it can exist. Like Goldilocks, most organisms thrive in places that aren't too hot or too cold. They need the right amount of water, sunlight, and oxygen to survive.

In 2016, scientists will be aiming at history once again by landing an unmanned probe on an asteroid, and then watching as it returns to Earth with a sample of dirt. Scientists hope to answer a number of questions about how our solar system formed when OSIRIS-REx encounters the asteroid named Bennu.

Bennu is unlike most asteroids, which orbit an area called the Asteroid Belt between Mars and Jupiter. Bennu, which is longer than four football fields, orbits near Earth, making it a good target to study.

Scientists say asteroids are leftovers of a giant cloud of gas and dust that created the sun, the planets, and moons some 4.5 billion years ago. Many believe these interstellar rocks seeded Earth with organic compounds, giving rise to the first life forms on the planet. Bennu is a **carbonaceous** asteroid, which means it contains a wide range of organic mol-

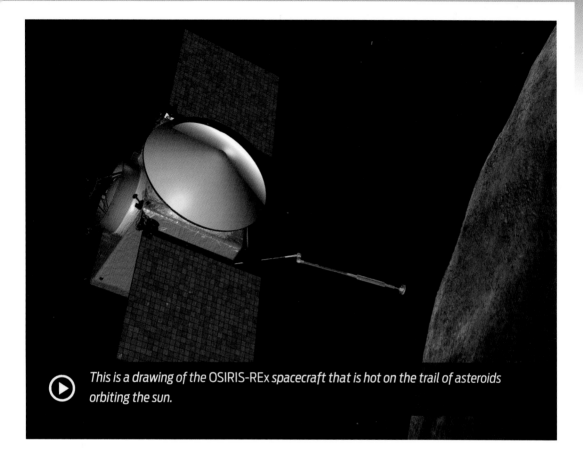

This is a drawing of the OSIRIS-REx spacecraft that is hot on the trail of asteroids orbiting the sun.

ecules such as amino acids, which have been found in samples of meteorites and comets.

The solar-powered *OSIRIS-REx* began its journey in 2016 and chased Bennu around the sun. It won't be easy to catch up to Bennu because the asteroid is flying through the solar system at an average of 63,000 miles (101,388 km) per hour. When *OSIRIS-REx* finds Bennu, it will look for the best place to land. Once it does, it will begin its descent with its robotic arm outstretched. That arm, the Touch-and-Go Same Acquisition Mechanism, will touch the surface of the asteroid for about five seconds. During

*This composite and computer-colored image shows Alpha Centauri, our nearest star neighbor in the Milky Way, only 50,000 years of travel away!*

that brief period, the arm will release a burst of nitrogen gas to stir up the soil and rocks and pick up about 2.1 ounces (59.5 g) of dirt and debris. *OSIRIS-REx* will then make its way back to Earth and deliver its package sometime in 2019.

## To the Stars, and Beyond

While unmanned space probes provide researchers with the best science, only one has ever left the solar system. Launched in 1977, Voyager 1 left the sun's gravitational influence in 2012. The trip took 35 years.

Scientists are working hard to reduce the time it takes to travel through deep space. One program is known as Project Icarus. Its mission will be one day to travel to another star, quite possibly Alpha Centauri.

As you read before, it would take about 50,000 years to travel to Alpha Centauri using today's technology. Scientists hope to shorten travel time to just 50 years. To accomplish such a feat, scientists say they would have to build a ship that can fly along at 10 percent the speed of light. Light travels at 186,000 miles per second—or about a 1,000 times faster than any ship has ever gone. As it makes its journey, the Icarus starship will pick up velocity by making close passes to planets in our solar system. Spaceships do this all the time. It's called the "slingshot effect."

## [?] Text-Dependent Questions

1. Explain how a Huntsville Nuclear Cryogenic Propulsion system would work.

2. What is the difference between fission and fusion?

3. What space probe has ever left the solar system?

## Research Project

Research and create a visual timeline of human rocketry from the 20th century to now.

The powerful, multi-stage Orion rocket blasts off from a launching pad in Florida. Orion is the centerpiece of NASA's growing plans for a manned mission to Mars.

# ENGINEERING AND
# Space

## Words to Understand

**cataclysmic**   devastating

**infrared**   having a wavelength just greater than that of the red end of the visible light spectrum

**micrometeoroids**   very small dust particles found in space that land on Earth or the moon

**sensors**   devices capable of detecting and responding to such things as movement, light, or heat

At 7:05 A.M. on December 5, 2014, the early morning sky over South Florida exploded in a brilliant plume of fire and smoke. Scientists and engineers kept their collective fingers crossed as a Delta IV rocket blasted off from Cape Canaveral Air Force Station carrying the future of human spaceflight. Sitting on top of the rocket was a 19,000-pound [8,618 kg] spacecraft named *Orion*, which scientists hope will one day take humans to the moon and beyond.

A Space Launch System will soon carry this crew capsule into space as part of ongoing tests of the rocket and its capabilities.

The launch was a test flight, the first time the capsule had flown into outer space. *Orion* made two orbits around the globe, reaching an altitude of more than 3,000 miles (4,828 m). It splashed down in the Pacific Ocean just outside San Diego four hours later. At one point, *Orion* streaked along at 20,000 miles (32,186 km) per hour.

Once it was back on Earth, engineers and technicians poured through data collected by **sensors** aboard the capsule. They designed the flight to test the capsule's heat shield, which protects the craft from the immense heat generated by reentry into the atmosphere. Engineers also looked at how the ship's guidance, parachute-deployment, and computer systems worked.

## Engineering Marvel

As *Orion* orbited the planet, other engineers were busily building a more powerful rocket that will propel the capsule way beyond Earth's orbit, perhaps to Mars. That rocket will stand taller than the Statue of Liberty and create 8.4 million pounds of thrust, which is equal to 135 Boeing 747 jet engines firing at once.

Engineers at NASA and Lockheed Martin, the company building the Space Launch System, hope the first manned flight will take place in 2021. They face enormous challenges. If *Orion* is to shuttle humans back and forth from Earth to the moon and Mars, engineers have to design the craft so that it doesn't weigh a lot but can carry the maximum amount of supplies, tools, and other cargo a six-person crew will need on a deep-space voyage. To that end, engineers are designing the spacecraft with the latest innovations in propulsion, safety, and other elements.

## Complex Field

*Orion* underscores the complex nature of engineering machines that will operate hundreds of thousands of miles in harsh and dangerous conditions. Every successful space mission, regardless of its scope, has a scientific mission at its core, and *Orion* is no exception. It is the engineer's job to meet each mission requirement, on time and on budget.

One of the biggest challenges engineers and technicians have is keeping a machine aloft in space, whether it is orbiting Earth or flying toward Venus. The International Space Station (ISS), for example, is the most complicated space-engineering job in human history and the largest structure ever put into space. Engineers are constantly updating and repairing the station, solving complex problems such as replacing failed components or repairing systems that have broken down. Engineers once had to figure out how astronauts could replace a computer system on the outside of the craft. In another instance, a crew had to fix a broken cooling line.

Engineers are constantly updating the craft and are currently trying to prepare the ISS for commercial spacecraft, which will begin arriving in 2017. Two new docking adaptors have to be added to the station.

### Engineering Miracle

Building the ISS, which is the size of a football field and weighs 827,794 pounds (375,480 kg), was an engineering miracle. To get such a massive structure into space, engineers from five different space agencies in 15 countries had to build and assemble the ISS one piece at a time like a giant, orbiting Lego set. Each module had to connect to one another. Engineers had to design living quarters, laboratories, structural supports, and massive solar panels. Humans have occupied the ISS since November 2000.

## Moon Base

Humans have mastered living high above the Earth, orbiting in space stations such as Skylab, Mir, and the ISS. However, astronauts have not spent any great amount of time living beyond their home

This image from Apollo 12's mission in late 1969 shows an astronaut investigating the dusty surface of the moon.

planet. Scientists hope to change that by one day building a human colony on the moon. Space officials in Europe, the United States, and China are trying to find ways to build a lunar base to provide humans with a cosmic bus stop on the way to Mars.

The moon is brimming with large amounts of water, ice, and other useful compounds. All of these resources, scientists think, can be used to build and maintain a space base. Engineers working for the European Space Agency have already begun to design what a moon base could look like. They plan to use 3D printing technology to create habitats that will ward off radiation and are be able to deflect incoming objects, such as tiny meteors.

*Imagination: Just how a moon base might look remains a mystery, but scientists and artists are coming up with numerous ideas for such a human habitat.*

One plan is to inflate an igloo-like bladder that will be used as a skeleton for a permanent habitat. Over the course of three months, a 3D printing robot, which looks like a vacuum cleaner on tank treads, will roll across the lunar surface sucking up piles of moon dust. The 'bot will combine the dust with magnesium oxide, then spit out pulp-like blocks. Once the blocks are formed, the robot will apply a salt that hardens and binds them together.

Like a mechanical bricklayer, the robot will lay, or print, the blocks around the bladder, layer after honey-combed layer, until the building is finished. When completed, the outside walls will be able to withstand impacts from **micrometeoroids** and shield those inside from radiation.

Engineers say the structure could be ready for human occupation three months after the 3D 'bot lands on the moon. The interior of the bladder shell will become a living and working space. It will have two floors and a laboratory.

Another plan calls for building a permanent base by using inflatable modules. Since the moon is hammered every day with dangerous levels of radiation, the inflatable homes would need to be buried in large tubes underground or covered with lunar

### Far Side of the Moon

The Chinese want to build a lunar base on the far side of the moon, which never faces Earth. They expect to land a ship and robotic rover in the region sometime in 2018 to 2019. The probe will be accompanied by a relay satellite that will orbit the moon sending signals back to Earth. The rover will explore the surface and send back information so scientists and engineers can decide whether the far side of the moon is an appropriate place to build a base.

soil. Engineers are testing a hybrid module—one that is rigid but has an inflatable top—in the desert of Arizona.

## Eye Spy

The Hubble Space Telescope has been orbiting high above Earth for nearly 30 years, sending back amazing images of outer space. It has seen the birth of stars thousands of light years away and spotted numerous galaxies. It has helped scientists figure out how planets formed.

Engineers and scientists always knew Hubble would not last forever, so they designed a much more powerful telescope that will dwarf the accomplishments of Hubble. The new James Webb Telescope (named after a former NASA administrator) will be three times as large as Hubble and a hundred times more powerful. "Going from Hubble to the James Webb Space Telescope is like going from a biplane to the jet engine," one U.S. senator said.

Built by NASA, the European Space Agency, the Canadian Space Agency, the University of Arizona, and Lockheed Martin, Webb will be able to look back 13 billion years to about the time the universe was born in a great explosion called the Big Bang. That is the name of the **cataclysmic** explosion that created time, space, the planets, the stars, and, ultimately…us.

Up close with the Hubble Space Telescope

Because it takes time for the light of distant objects to reach Earth, Webb will, in

Technicians work on just a few of the many enormous mirrors that will be part of the Webb Space Telescope that might just change how we think about the universe.

reality, be studying nearly every moment of the history of the universe. It will be able to look back to the first light generated by the Big Bang. It will be able to see the first galaxies or other luminous objects formed during the great explosion. Webb will help scientists figure out how galaxies evolved and how stars and planets formed.

At the heart of Webb is a 21.3-foot (6.5 m) mirror, which engineers designed with 18 hexagonal segments. It will be the

## Time- and Money Saver

In 2015, NASA engineers were able to make a copper rocket-engine part using a 3D printer. Rockets involve millions of complex parts, and each has to be made in different ways. 3D printers, engineers say, can do the same type of work in less time and for less money. To make the copper engine part, engineers used a special, laser 3D printer. It was able to fuse 8,255 layers of copper powder to make the part in only 10 days and 18 hours.

"Our goal is to build rocket engine parts up to ten times faster and reduce cost by more than fifty percent," said NASA engineer Chris Protz. "We are not trying to just make and test one part. We are developing a repeatable process that industry can adopt to manufacture engine parts with advanced designs. The ultimate goal is to make building rocket engines more affordable for everyone."

largest mirror ever launched into space. Building the mirror was so complex that engineers had to invent new machines to measure the lens during manufacturing. They also had to find a way to make sure the mirrors could hold up in the extremely cold temperatures in outer space.

## Invisible Light

Webb will use its gigantic lens to capture infrared light, which the human eye cannot see. The telescope will peek through seemingly impenetrable clouds of dust. Webb will not actually orbit Earth as Hubble does. Instead, it will park itself 932,056 miles (1.5 million km) into space, nearly twice as far as the moon.

Because Webb's mirror is so large, it can collect more light from objects, just as a bucket collects more water than a paper cup. The mirror will allow Webb to see very detailed images of distant objects, including "baby galaxies," born right after the Big Bang.

One reason an infrared telescope such as Webb will be able to spot these first galaxies is because soon after the Big Bang, these clusters of stars began moving away from each other. The most distant galaxies are the youngest and they are moving away so fast that the light they emit is redder than other galaxies. Engineers also installed a shield on the telescope to block light from Earth, the moon, and the sun. This will help Webb keep cool and not overheat.

 # Text-Dependent Questions

1. What was the top speed of the *Orion* space capsule during its first test flight?

2. How much more powerful will the James Webb Telescope be than the Hubble Space Telescope?

3. Explain how some engineers plan to build a lunar base using 3D printers.

 # Research Project

Write a fictional story about a futuristic space mission. Make sure you create characters that move the story along. Give the reader at least one character he or she can root for. Make sure that every sentence either reveals some aspect of a character or advances the action. The story should have a beginning, middle, and an end.

What's next? The future of interstellar travel

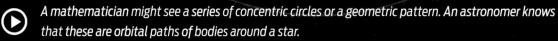

*A mathematician might see a series of concentric circles or a geometric pattern. An astronomer knows that these are orbital paths of bodies around a star.*

# MATH AND
# Space

## Words to Understand

**astronomers**   scientists who study stars, moons, galaxies, and other objects

**drag**   the resistance to the motion of a moving object through water or air

**mass**   the measure of the amount of matter an object contains and its influence in a gravitational field

Space is a curious place. It seems empty, but it's not. It seems like stars and planets aren't moving, but they are. Engineers, physicists, **astronomers**, astronauts, and others rely on math to find out how things work in outer space.

Engineers use math to build spaceships. Astronomers use math to calculate distances between stars. Astronauts use math to grab hold of a satellite slated for repair or to dock with a space station.

The International Space Station orbits the Earth about once every 90 minutes, flying at 17,000 miles (28,000 km) per hour.

It would take too many pages to tell you all the ways people use math to understand outer space, but you should know that without math, humans would simply look at the stars and wonder how and why.

## Package Drop Off

Math plays a crucial role when spaceships meet up with each other. In July 2015, an unmanned Russian spacecraft blasted off from Baikonur Cosmodrome in Kazakhstan, carrying 6,100 pounds (2,766 kg) of food, water, oxygen, fuel, and other supplies for the International Space Station. Unlike a delivery truck dropping off packages at your house, transporting cargo to a space station orbiting Earth is a complex job. It can only be accomplished by calculating thousands of mathematical equations.

The ISS is always on the go. It orbits Earth at 17,000 (28,000 km) miles per hour. A supply ship coming from Earth is moving, too. Both move according to the laws of orbital mechanics, the study of how artificial satellites and space vehicles move under the influence of gravity, atmospheric drag, and thrust.

Eventually, the supply ship has to catch up to the ISS to deliver the supplies. To make sure that happens at the right moment, scientists have to figure out the orbital velocities and position of both space vehicles. It's like throwing a Frisbee to a running dog. Both are in motion at different rates of speed. Eventually the two must end up at the same place at the same time for the dog to catch the Frisbee.

## The Long Way Home

On Earth, the shortest distance between two points is a straight line. In space, things are much different. Space is not

## Newton in Orbit

The roots of orbital mechanics began with the great 17th century thinker Isaac Newton. He envisioned placing a cannon at the summit of a high mountain way above the effect of atmospheric **drag**.

In his mind's eye, Newton fired his theoretical cannon. The cannonball flew out of the weapon in an arc, falling to the ground as Earth's gravity tugged on it. Newton thought that if he packed the cannon with more gunpowder, the cannonball would fly faster and farther from the mountain while falling to Earth at the same rate as the first cannonball.

Newton then wondered what would happen if he packed the cannon with even more gunpowder. He believed the cannonball would fly so much faster and farther than the previous cannonballs that it would never have a chance to touch down.

He concluded that the last cannonball would fall toward Earth just as fast as Earth curved away from it. He said the cannonball would continue forever in an orbit around the planet. His thought experiment provided modern-day scientists with the principle for space travel.

flat like a piece of paper. Space is curved because of the gravitational influence of galaxies, planets, and stars. Like a bowling ball tossed into the middle of a trampoline, gravity warps, or bends, space. That's the reason why planets revolve around stars, and moons revolve around planets.

Over the years, mathematicians and engineers have found ways to use gravity to send ships rocketing through space without using much fuel. In 2004, NASA launched its *Genesis* spacecraft to grab solar particles from the sun and bring them back to Earth. The spacecraft traveled to a point between the Earth and sun where the gravitational influence of both is balanced. It's called the Lagrange Point.

*Genesis* did what it had to do, but it did not come straight home. Instead, it took a 1 million-mile, circular route back to Earth, even going past the planet once. The path allowed *Genesis* to use gravity to push it along without using any fuel.

## Warp Speed

The starship *Enterprise* was one of the fastest spaceships around. It could fly between star systems at warp speed, which was much faster than the speed of light. The only problem is that both the *Enterprise* and warp speed existed only in the minds of the writers who created the TV show (and later movies) *Star Trek*.

But Geraint Lewis, from the University of Sydney in Australia, believes humans can break the universal speed limit and, one day, travel between galaxies. How can that be? The great physicist Albert Einstein said nothing moves faster than light. Yet, it is Einstein's theories, Lewis said, that will make warp speed possible.

In 1905, Einstein came up with what he called his special theory of relativity. It is the most famous equation in science: $E = mc^2$. *E* stands for energy, *m* for **mass**, and *c* for the speed of light. The equation means that the energy contained in any object is equal to its mass multiplied by the speed of light squared—a huge number. With that equation, Einstein showed that mass and energy can be changed into one another. It also suggested that nothing can travel faster than the speed of light.

However, Einstein came up with another theory in 1919—the theory of general relativity. In that theory, which was based on a number of mathematical equations, gravity bends both space and time, just like the bowling ball on the trampoline.

It is Einstein's general theory of relativity, Lewis said, that provides a way to make warp speed possible. "It shows you can bend and warp space so you can travel at any speed you like in the universe," Lewis said.

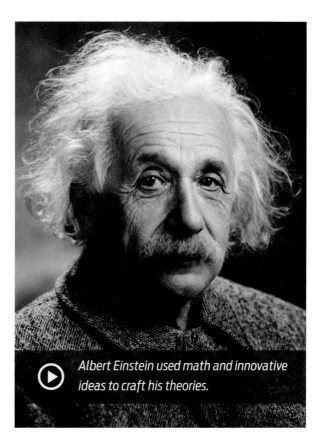

*Albert Einstein used math and innovative ideas to craft his theories.*

The problem is that we would need special materials and an enormous amount of energy to warp space and time—technology that we do not yet have. NASA scientists say motoring around the universe faster than the speed of light can't be done—yet.

"Science fiction writers have given us many images of interstellar travel, but traveling at the speed of light is simply imaginary at present," the agency concluded. "There are many 'absurd' theories that have become reality over the years of scientific research. But for the near future, warp drive remains a dream."

*Room for one more? The SpaceX private craft was hired by NASA to deliver supplies to the ISS, but in the future, it might take tourists into space.*

Space science is all about dreams, as well as understanding the amazing reality of space. Using science, people on Earth explore the heavens. Technology and engineering give them the tools to make those journeys. Math helps explain the principles guiding space and space travel. We are all voyagers on a planet moving through the vast universe. STEM subjects give us the guidebook we need to understand the journey.

 **Text-Dependent Questions**

1. Name each aspect of orbital mechanics.

2. What does the equation $E = mc^2$ mean?

3. What does Einstein call space and time?

 **Research Project**

Write a short biography of Albert Einstein, Edwin Hubble, or Isaac Newton.

# Find Out More

## Books

Aguilar, David. *Space Encyclopedia: A Tour of Our Solar System and Beyond.* Washington, D.C.: National Geographic for Kids, 2013.

Miller Ron. *Rockets (Space Innovations).* Minneapolis, Minn.: Twenty-First Century Books, 2007.

Rogers, Lucy. *It's ONLY Rocket Science.* New York: Springer, 2008.

Wallace, Karen. *Rockets and Space Ships.* New York: DK Readers, 2001.

## Websites

European Space Agency
*www.esa.int/ESA*

NASA: Kennedy Space Center
*www.nasa.gov/centers/kennedy/about/history/spacehistory_toc.html*

NASA Kids' Club
*www.nasa.gov/audience/forkids/kidsclub/flash/index.html*

Solar System Exploration
*solarsystem.nasa.gov/index.cfm*

# Series Glossary of Key Terms

**capacity**   the amount of a substance that an object can hold or transport

**consumption**   the act of using a product, such as electricity

**electrodes**   a material, often metal, that carries electrical current into or out of a nonmetallic substance

**evaporate**   to change from a liquid to a gas

**fossil fuels**   a fuel in the earth that formed long ago from dead plants and animals

**inorganic**   describing materials that do not contain the element carbon

**intermittently**   not happening in a regular or reliable way

**ion**   an atom or molecule containing an uneven number of electrons and protons, giving a substance either a positive or negative charge

**microorganism**   a tiny living creature visible only under a microscope

**nuclear**   referring to the nucleus, or center, of an atom, or the energy that can be produced by splitting or joining together atoms

**organic**   describing materials or life forms that contain the element carbon; all living things on Earth are organic

**piston**   part of an engine that moves up and down in a tube; its motion causes other parts to move

**prototype**   the first model of a device used for testing; it serves as a design for future models or a finished product

**radiation**   a form of energy found in nature that, in large quantities, can be harmful to living things

**reactor**   a device used to carry out a controlled process that creates nuclear energy

**sustainable**   able to be used without being completely used up, such as sunlight as an energy source

**turbines**   an engine with large blades that turn as liquids or gases pass over them

**utility**   a company chosen by a local government to provide an essential product, such as electricity

# Index

3D Ice House 11

3D printing 9, 10, 11, 49, 52

Alpha Centauri 41

Ames Research Center 18

asteroids 37, 38

DNA 20, 21, 23, 24, 25

Dyson, Freeman 35

Einstein, Albert 59, 60

Genesis 58

Hawking, Stephen 22

Hubble Space Telescope 15, 50

Huntsville Nuclear Cryogenic Propulsion Stage Team 32, 35

International Space Station 24, 46, 57

Kelly, Mark 24

Kelly, Scott 24

Kepler Space Telescope 27, 38

Lockheed Martin 45

Mars 7, 8, 9, 11, 19, 20, 32, 36

Mars Reconnaissance Orbiter (MRO) 7, 8, 9

math and space 55–60

McKay, Chris 17, 18, 19, 20

Moon base 46, 47, 49

NASA 22, 32, 34, 45, 50, 52, 58, 60

Newton, Isaac 57

Osiris-REX 38, 39

Pluto 20

Project Icarus 40, 41

Project Orion 35, 43, 44, 45

rockets 31, 32

SETI (Search for Exterrestrial Intelligence) 28

Sfrero 9, 10

solar sails 36

terraforming 17, 18, 19

Venus 19

"vomit comet" 22, 23, 24

Voyager 1 40

Webb Space Telescope 50, 51

# Credits

NASA/JPL-Caltech/Univ. of Arizona 6, 8; Fabulous.com/Studio Charles Bel 11; John Frassanito and Associates for NASA 12; NASA/Hubble 14, 18; Daein Ballard/Wiki 16; NASA/JPL-Caltech 17, 54; NASA 21, 25, 26, 30, 33, 44, 46, 48, 51, 56, 60; NASA/Jim Campbell/Aero-News Network 22; Courtesy ATA 28; University of Washington MSNW 34; ESO 40; Bill Ingalls/NASA 42; Library of Congress 60.

# About the Author

**John Perritano** is an award-winning journalist, writer, and editor from Southbury, Conn., who has written numerous articles and books on a variety of subjects, including science, sports, history, and culture for such publishers as National Geographic, Scholastic, and Time/Life. His articles have appeared on Discovery.com, Popular Mechanics.com, and other magazines and websites. He holds a master's degree in American History from Western Connecticut State University.